A to Z: Your Grand County History Alphabet

By Penny Rafferty Hamilton, Ph.D.

Grand County Historical Association

Book Cover photographs clockwise:
      Saturday Night Bath (GCHA archive)
      Ute mother and baby (Library of Congress)
      Racing Stagecoach (GCHA archive)
      Train station donkeys (GCHA archive)
      Welcome to Grand County (Hamilton collection)

Graphic Design by Patricia Shapiro
      Some modified graphics provided by 123rf.com

Grand County Historical Association
PO Box 165
110 East Byers Avenue
Hot Sulphur Springs, CO 80451-0165
(970) 725-3939
www.GrandCountyHistory.org

ISBN-13: 978-0-692-83321-6

HOWDY!

History Readers,

Grand County is in colorful Colorado. In Spanish, Colorado means "colored red." Many years ago, Native Americans lived here. Later, rugged Mountain Men, fur trappers, & prospectors came. Some helped the United States Government map what became Grand County.

In 1874, Grand County was created, even before Colorado became a State. Our meadows, rivers, & mountains attracted loggers, ranchers, store, and hotel owners. The Moffat Railroad brought even more people. Soon our towns changed and grew. Today, those places are named Fraser, Granby, Grand Lake, Hot Sulphur Springs, Kremmling, Parshall, Radium, Tabernash, & Winter Park. This book shares our pioneer story.

All of these people helped: Becky Arnold, Steve Batty, Elin Capps, Jill Childress, Donald Dailey, Doug Doubek, Linda Gillogley, Dave Lively, Patty Madison, Joy McCoy, Sheridan Myer, Mary Jane Peace, Middle Park Cowbelles, Katlin Miller, Sandra Pedersen, Tess Riley, Kari Simmons, Michele Simmons, Rita Snock, Jane Tollett, Town of Fraser, YMCA of the Rockies, Tammy Yurich, Kathie Yost, and Jim Yust. Other book helpers are on the alphabet pages.

A special thank you to Dan Nolan, Tim Nicklas, Dr. William Hamilton, & Dr. Kristi Martens for their guidance. Graphic artist, Patricia Shapiro, created the pages. The Bessie Minor Swift Foundation helped fund this book.

Your new history friend,

Dr. Penny

AIRPLANES & AIRPORTS

First airplane & pilot to land in Kremmling. (GCHA archive)

First airplane & pilot to land in Tabernash. (GCHA archive)

In 1903, the Wright brothers' airplane changed the world. Can you say "AIRPLANE?"

Brave pilots, called "Barnstormers," landed airplanes in fields near barns.

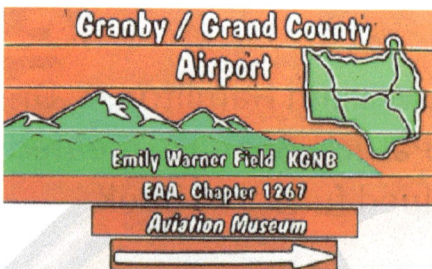

In 1945, Granby/Grand County Airport officially opened. (Hamilton collection)

Granby's Emily Warner is America's FIRST female airline captain. (Warner collection)

In 1946, Kremmling airport opened on land donated by the Henry McElroy family. (Hamilton collection)

B

Middle Park
Stockgrowers Association

Brands of Grand & Summit Counties

Keeping Agriculture Alive

The Sheriff Ranch Bar Double S brand began in 1881. Can you find their Bar SS brand?

U on its side is called a "Lazy U." The C Lazy U brand is easy to read. (Hamilton collection)

Can you draw a brand on a cupcake? (Hamilton collection)

Unique brands, listed in The Colorado Brand Book, mark ranch animals to show ownership.

C COZENS RANCH

In 1876, Billy Cozens was the first Fraser Postmaster. At the Cozens Stagecoach Stop, tired, hungry travelers were fed by Mary & her daughters. (GCHA archive)

In 1874, Pioneers, Billy & Mary Cozens, homesteaded the very first Fraser Valley ranch. Can you say "PIONEER?"

The Cozens Family built a six-bedroom home used as a hotel, horse corrals, and barns for their 700-acre ranch. (GCHA archive)

D

Fraser's Doctor Susan Anderson helped everyone. For healing his dog, the late Chuck Orlunsky painted Doc Susie's picture. (Vickie Simpson photo)

Kremmling's Doctor Ernest Ceriani often walked to the homes of sick people to help them. (GCHA archive)

A Doctor is a person trained to help and heal. Other longer names are physician, dentist, and veterinarian

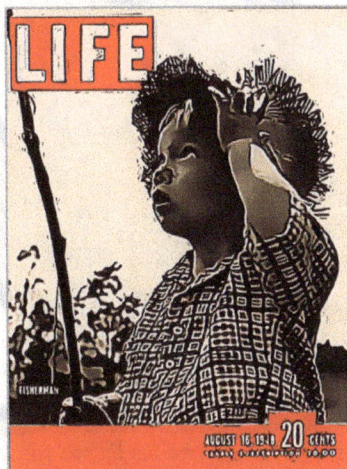

In 1948, Life Magazine featured Country Doctor Ceriani's story.

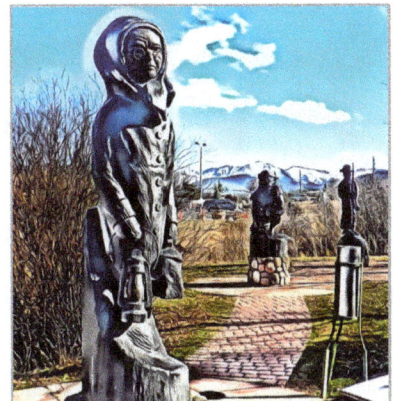

In 1907, Doc Susie arrived by train. Her statue in the Fraser Walk Through History reminds us of this remarkable woman. (Hamilton collection)

E

Eisenhower's fishing trips are remembered with this Fraser Valley Lions Club bronze statue. (Gary Schoen, Schoen Photography)

Winter Park's Jean & Dwight Miller's daughter, Martha, met President Eisenhower and reporters. (GCHA archive)

United States President Dwight Eisenhower loved fishing while visiting Fraser's Byers Peak Ranch.

President Eisenhower described his fly rod to residents gathered around him. (GCHA archive)

F FOREST

A forest is land with lots & lots of trees. Say "FOREST."

The US Forest Service & Colorado State Forest Service promote healthy forests.

In early 1900, the Williams Fork River Valley US Forest Service Horseshoe Ranger Station was important. (GCHA archive)

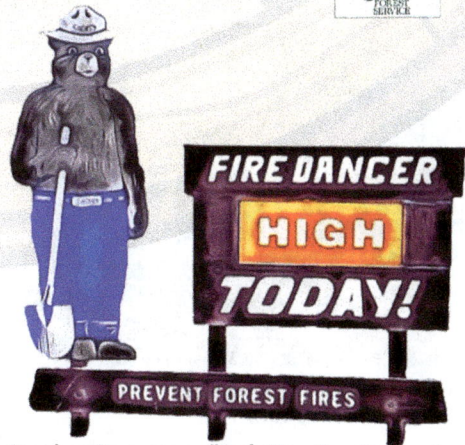

Smokey Bear says, "Only You Can Prevent Forest Fires."

Rangers check on Arapaho National Forest tools. James Buchholz was one of our first Grand County US Forest Service Rangers. (Library of Congress)

G

The Denver, Northwestern & Pacific Railroad named Granby after their lawyer, Granby Hillyer.

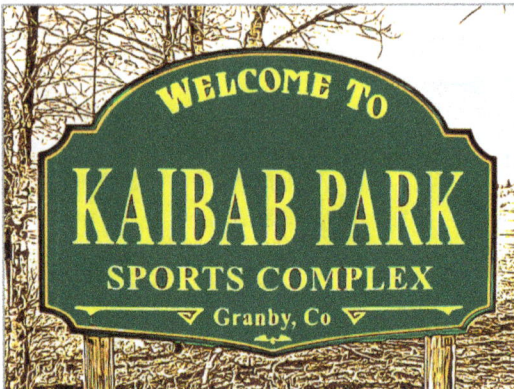

Kaibab (sounds like KY-BAB) is a Native American word. (Hamilton collection)

The Tovey Stage Line & an early car met Granby train passengers around 1911. (GCHA archive)

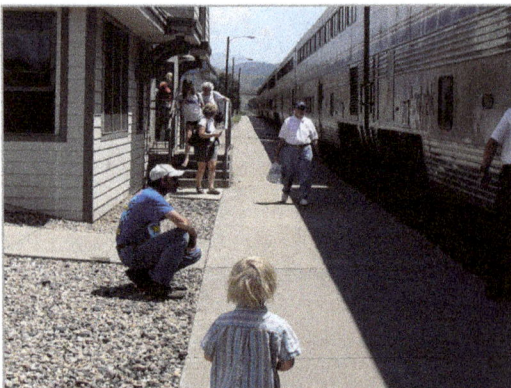

The Granby train station at 439 Railroad Avenue still welcomes travelers today. (Patrick Brower)

In the 1920s, Granby was "The Lettuce Capital" because Granby lettuce was served in expensive restaurants nationwide. (GCHA archive)

G

Pioneer Judge Joseph Wescott built Grand Lake's first cabin.

Welcome To
Historic
Grand Lake
Est. 1881

MT. BALDY
FROM GRAND LAKE, COLO.

Grand Lake is Colorado's largest natural lake. Mount Craig is called "Mount Baldy" because its top looks bald. (GCHA archive)

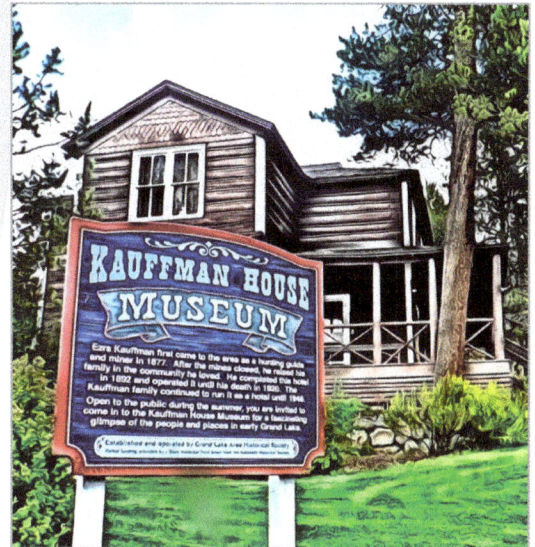

KAUFFMAN HOUSE
MUSEUM

The Kauffman House hotel started in 1892. Visit the museum to learn how real pioneers lived. (Hamilton collection)

Grand Lake was always a very popular tourist stop. (GCHA archive)

H

Long before William Byers named the town in 1874, Native Americans called the hot springs "healing waters."

Hot Sulphur Springs
First in Winter Carnivals
ELEV 7670 FEET

In the early 1900s, the first Hot Sulphur Springs Resort pool house was built. (GCHA Archive)

In 1905, David Moffat's railroad finally reached Hot Sulphur Springs. (GCHA archive)

Since 1888, Grand County government & the Courthouse have been in Hot Sulphur Springs, making it the County Seat. (Hamilton collection)

In 1911, Hot Sulphur Springs hosted Colorado's first Winter Sports Carnival. (GCHA archive)

In 1978, Congress created our Indian Peaks Wilderness as a natural, protected area within the Arapaho National Forest.

Lone Eagle Peak is named after famous aviator, Charles Lindbergh. (GCHA archive)

Called Lone Eagle, Lindbergh flew his historic 1927 flight alone. (Library of Congress)

Many years ago, Native Americans lived in the wilderness. Today, most of the Indian Peaks have names to honor them as Apache Peak, Kiowa Peak, and Pawnee Peak.

J

A ski jump is a snow-covered slide or chute. Ski jumpers race down it on long skis & jump into the air, almost flying.

Winter Park ski jumpers, Landis Arnold & Todd Wilson, jumped in the Olympics.

Norwegian Carl Howelsen was called "The Flying Norseman" at the 1911 & 1912 Hot Sulphur Springs Winter Sports Carnivals. (GCHA archive)

Hot Sulphur Springs' Barney McLean, taught by Horace Button, soared to be 9-time National Champion and a three-time Olympic ski jumper. (GCHA archive)

In 1911, Hot Sulphur Springs' Horace Button, age ten, dedicated himself to be like Winter Sports Carnival Hero Carl Howelsen. With hard work, Horace became an All-American skier and coach (GCHA archive)

K

KREMMLING

Rudolph Kremmling's general store was the first business. Kremmling became the town's official name in 1895.

KREMMLING
A Sportsman's Paradise

In 1908, Henry McElroy's Livery & Feed & a stagecoach service started. Later, Henry & Lillie donated land for the Middle Park Fair & Rodeo. (GCHA archive)

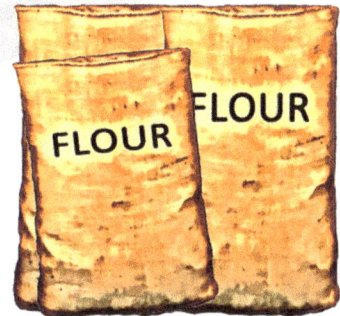

FLOUR FLOUR

FARM PRODUCE

In July 1906, the Moffat Railroad arrived. Kremmling became the central shipping point. (GCHA archive)

L

FRASER COLORADO

With the arrival of the railroad in 1904, Scandinavian immigrants logged the forests. George Eastom built the first lumber mill in the town of Fraser.

In Fraser, one Swedish logger holds a kitten, another a music squeeze box, the others display logging items--a hammer, axe, wood barking tool, & a big log saw. (GCHA archive)

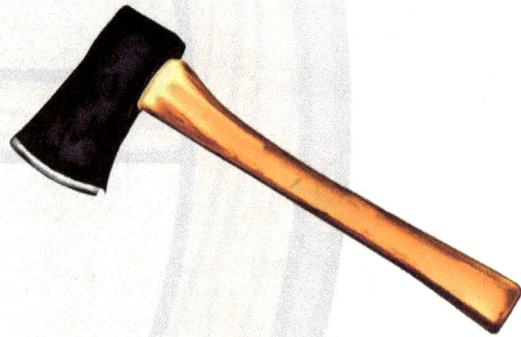

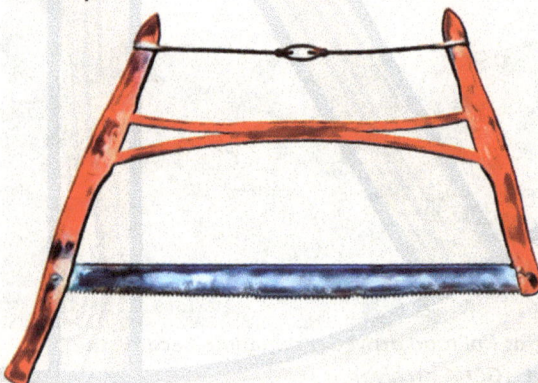

After the skilled loggers cut down the big trees, horses pulled heavy logs to the Fraser lumber mill. (GCHA archive)

MOUNTAIN PASS

UTE PASS SUMMIT ELEV 9165 FT

A Mountain Pass is an important route over a mountain.

COTTONWOOD PASS
ELEVATION 12,126 FEET
CONTINENTAL DIVIDE
ATLANTIC OCEAN | PACIFIC OCEAN
SAN ISABEL National Forest | GUNNISON National Forest

In the 1920s, the Berthoud Pass Inn served summer tourists riding horses & driving cars. (GCHA archive)

The Berthoud Pass Wagon Road opened in 1874. (GCHA archive)

Corona-Rollins Railroad Pass was the highest in North America. In 1904, the Corona Hotel was called "the top of the world." (GCHA archive)

NATIVE AMERICANS

The Utes hunted here. They made their tipis (teepees) from animal skins & pine poles. (Library of Congress)

To Arapahos, the "Ni-chebe-chii" mountains meant "Never No Summer." Today, known as "Never Summer Mountains." (Library of Congress)

Many years ago, Native Americans freely roamed the land. A few places reflect their history here.

Rocky Mountain National Park West Kawuneeche (Ka-wun nee chee) Visitor Center in Arapahoe means "valley of the coyote." (Rocky Mountain National Park)

OLYMPIANS

Olympians represent their country at the worldwide Winter or Summer Olympics held every four years.

III Olympic Winter Games

Grand Lake's Jim Harsh competed in the Nordic Combined.

Lake Placid, USA
February 4-13, 1932

Olympian John Cress represented the United States in Nordic Combined Ski.

VIII OLYMPIC WINTER GAMES CALIFORNIA 1960

Grand County's Landis Arnold, Kerry Lynch, Zane Palmer and Todd Wilson all are Winter Olympians too.

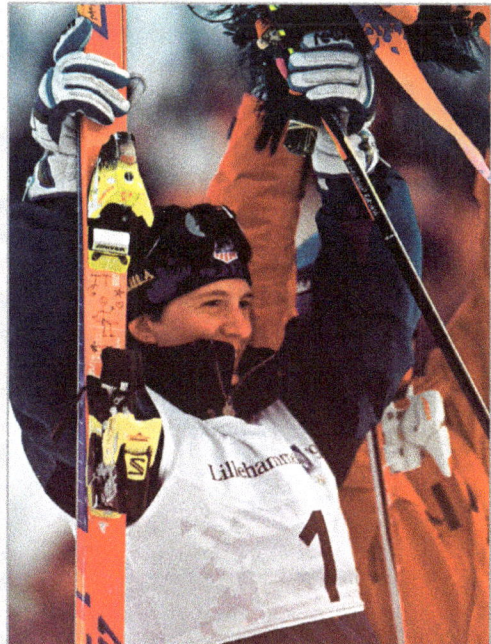

Winter Park's Liz McIntyre skied in the 1992, 1994, & 1998 Olympics, earning a silver medal for her mogul skiing. (GCHA archive)

Hot Sulphur Springs' Barney McLean, 3-time Olympian, was Captain of the 1948 men's alpine ski racing team. (GCHA archive)

P

PARSHALL

Parshall is named for engineer-inventor, Ralph Parshall, whose "Parshall Flume" water flow measuring device is used worldwide. In 1902, he bought land near the Grand & Williams Fork Rivers.

Ralph Parshall. (CSU archives)

In 1905, Walter Dow had a general store. The Parshall Post Office opened in 1906. In 1907, a hotel was built. (GCHA archive)

When the Moffat Railroad arrived, Parshall became an important cattle shipping & supply center. (GCHA archive)

Q

A Rodeo Queen represents the sport of rodeo. She wears a very special cowboy hat crown.

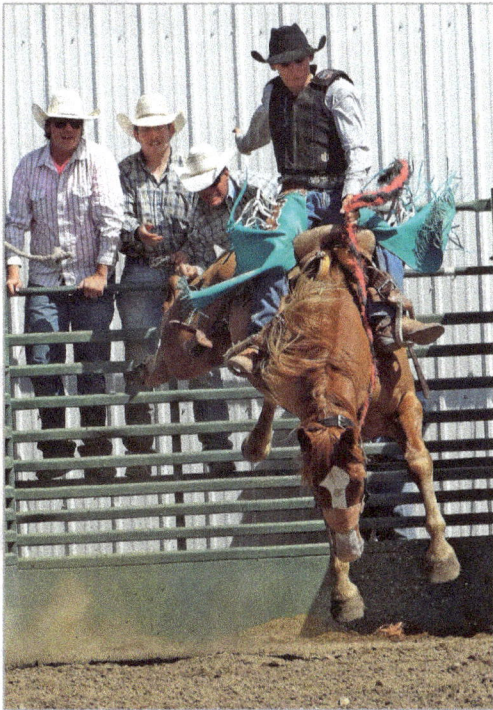

100th Middle Park Fair &Rodeo Queen, Meghan Cameron, is a skilled horse rider. (Hamilton collection)

Kremmling's Gavin McCallister won the Professional Rodeo Cowboys Association "Saddle Bronc" event at our 2016 Middle Park Fair. (Kim Cameron photo)

Middle Park Fair & Rodeo, over 100 years old, was the very first county fair in northwest Colorado. (Hamilton collection)

R

RANGER

A Ranger protects our
National Forests & Parks.

Wilderness, Wildlife, Wonder

Rocky Mountain National Park is
over 100 years old.

*Rangers understand nature. (Rocky Mountain
National Park)*

*YOU can become a Junior Ranger. (Rocky Mountain
National Park)*

R   RODEO

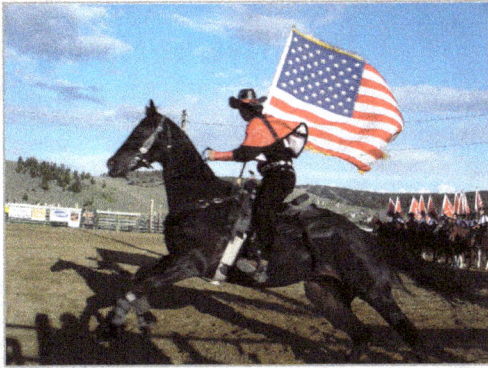

Granby's rodeo is at the Flying Heels Arena.
(www.granbyrodeo.com)

Fraser's rodeo is called High Country
Stampede. (GCHA archive)

On ranches, cowboys rode wild horses to tame
them. Rodeo bucking bronco events use those
same skills. (Cathie Hook)

A rodeo is an event featuring cowboy & cowgirl skills.

Roping cattle is another important ranching and rodeo skill.
(Cathie Hook)

S

Stores were often the first businesses in our towns.

In 1904, Fraser Mercantile sold food, shoes, & supplies. Guests rented 2nd floor rooms. (GCHA archive)

The Selak brothers sold fresh meat, eggs & "airtights" or canned goods. (GHCA archive)

In 1881, James Cairns opened the first Grand Lake General Store. Cairns Avenue & Cairns Peak honor him. (GCHA archive)

In 1906, Kremmling's Thomas J. Mitchell Hardware Store, known as the Winchester Building, opened. (GCHA archive)

S

STAGECOACH

Horses pulled the stagecoaches carrying mail, passengers, and even gold & silver. (GCHA archive)

In the 1890s, Walker McQueary's Hot Sulphur Springs Hotel was a stagecoach stop. (GCHA archive)

Pioneers traveled by stagecoach just as we do today by bus, train or airplane.

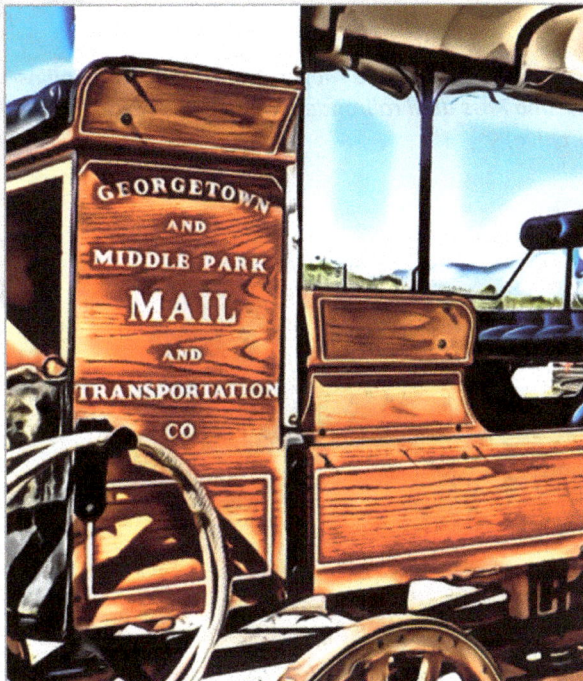

In 1903, Middle Park Mail stagecoaches covered Georgetown, Hot Sulphur Springs, and Grand Lake. (Hamilton collection)

In 1895, Dick & Jessie McQueary named their popular Georgetown Stage Line stop in Fraser 4 Bar 4, the same as their cattle brand. (GCHA archive)

T

TRAIN

A train is connected railroad cars pulled by a locomotive.

In 1905, train passengers rode David Moffat's Denver, Northwestern & Pacific Railroad to Hot Sulphur Springs. (GCHA archive)

Heavy snow stopped a Moffat train at the high Rollins-Corona Pass until railroaders cleared the track. (GCHA archive)

This is a modern freight train in Granby. (Hamilton collection)

Locomotives were called "Iron Horses." Why do you think they had that name? (GCHA archive)

U

Ute (sounds like YOOT), a Native American tribe lived in Grand County.

The Utes were the first tribe to have large horse herds. (Library of Congress)

In the early 1900s, the new town was named for Ute warrior, Tabernash, killed nearby in 1878. (Hamilton collection)

In the 1920s, Tabernash was on the Victory Highway, an important auto trail across America. (GCHA archive)

V

VISITORS

Visitors are guests. Grand County has guest ranches which welcome visitors from all over the world.

Opened in 1912, Bar Lazy J is Colorado's oldest continuously operating guest ranch. (Bar Lazy J Ranch)

Since 1919, C Lazy U Ranch is a world-wide favorite, with 5-Spur ratings. (Hamilton collection)

The Yagers started Devil's Thumb Ranch Resort. Now it a year-round destination. (Devil's Thumb Ranch, Resort & Spa)

Cowboy & cowgirl skills, roping & horses make Latigo Dude Ranch another Western favorite. (Latigo Ranch)

Drowsy Water is an award-winning, family resort almost 100 years old. (Hamilton collection)

W WINTER PARK

The Town of Winter Park & Winter Park Resort share history.

In 1978, the town became Winter Park. Early names were West Portal, Idlewild, Old Town, & Hideaway Park. (GCHA archive)

The City of Denver Winter Park Ski Area opened in December, 1939. (GCHA archive)

Skiers rode the Winter Park Ski Train from 1940-2009. (GCHA archive)

welcome to Downtown Winter Park

W

WHITE WATER

White water appears in rivers with rapids.

In 1927, the Colorado Legislature renamed the Grand River, the Colorado River. (Hamilton collection)

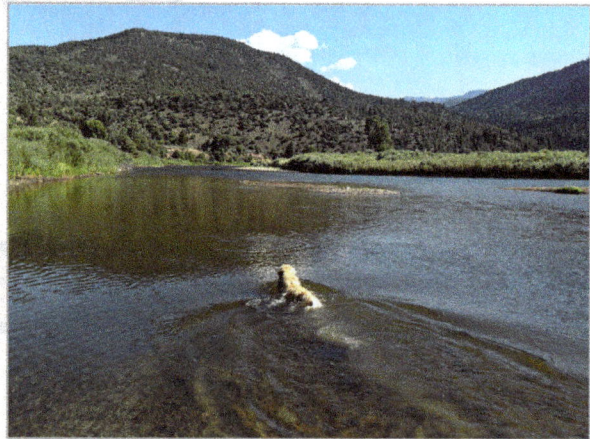

Radium Recreation Site offers river access and hot springs. (Lurline Curran)

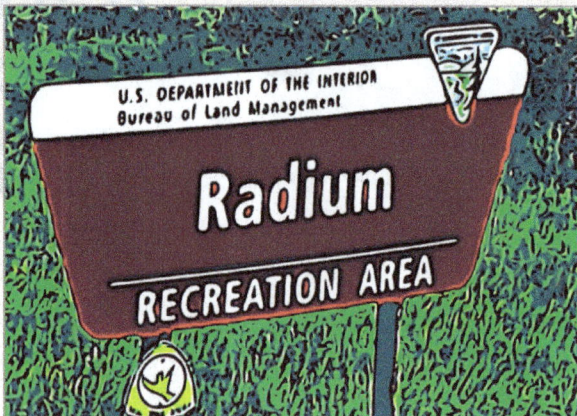

U.S. DEPARTMENT OF THE INTERIOR
Bureau of Land Management

Radium

RECREATION AREA

Harry Porter named Radium because of the radium in his mine nearby. (Bureau of Land Management)

88
Ra

88
Ra

88
Ra

The Colorado River, especially at Radium, has lots of white water for rafting. (Grand County Tourism Board)

e**X**plorers

Explorers venture into unknown and unmapped places.

Frontier Scout Jim Bridger's statue is in our Fraser History Walk. He guided many explorers. (Steve Sumrall photo)

Mountain Man, Harry Yount, on Berthoud Pass with the Hayden Survey mapping the West. (GCHA archive)

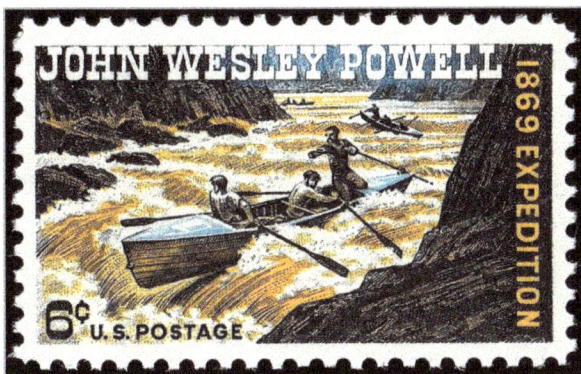

JOHN WESLEY POWELL
1869 EXPEDITION
6¢ U.S. POSTAGE

The Powell Expeditions explored our rivers. (US Postal Service)

Redwood Fisher surveyed with Edward Louis Berthoud for a route over the pass. (GCHA archive)

YMCA & YACHT CLUB

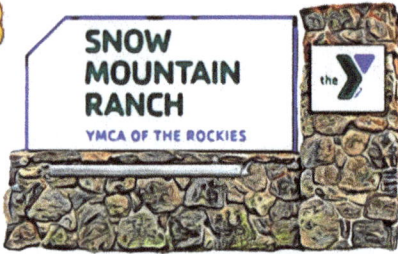

YMCA Snow Mountain Ranch offers nurturing for mind, body, and spirit.

Trapper's cabin from the Rowley Homestead. (GCHA archive)

The Rowley Homestead Interpretive Center is a living museum. (YMCA Snow Mountain Ranch)

The Grand Lake Yacht Club began in 1902. The Club House was built in 1912.

Grand Lake Yacht Club is the world's highest elevation registered yacht club. (GCHA archive)

Z

ZEPHYR & ZEREX

Zephyr (sounds like Zef er) means a West wind.

The fast train named Zephyr first stopped in Hot Sulphur Springs in 1934. (GCHA archive)

The California Zephyr still races through Grand County today. (Hamilton collection)

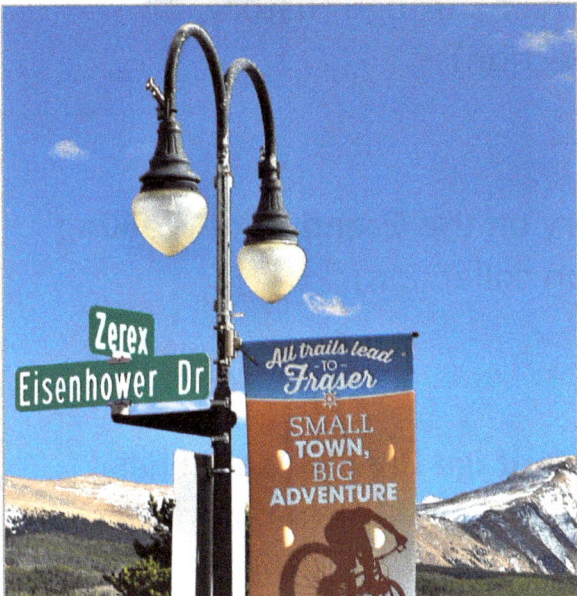

Fraser was called "Icebox of the Nation" so Zerex antifreeze was tested here. (Hamilton collection)

Z is also for Zerex Street.

FUN HISTORY PLACES TO EXPLORE

Cozens Ranch Museum is on the National Register of Historic Places. (Kristi Martens photo)

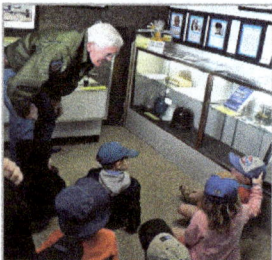

Emily Warner Field Aviation Museum is in the old Rocky Mountain Airways airline terminal. (Hamilton collection)

Mountain Man Jeremiah Johnson's statue is in the **Fraser Walk Through History**. (Hamilton Collection)

Discover history on the **Grand Lake Walking Tour**. (Hamilton collection)

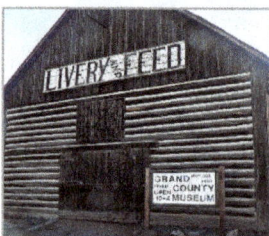

Kremmling's Heritage Park Museum has indoor & outdoor exhibits. (Hamilton collection)

MORE HISTORY PLACES

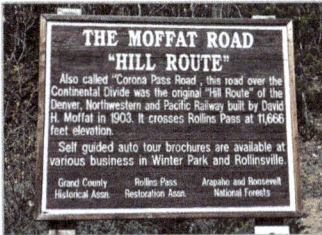

See where the pioneers on the **Moffat Railroad** rode. (Hamilton collection)

Pioneer Village Museum open in Hot Sulphur Springs all year. (Hamilton collection)

Explore more history in **Rocky Mountain National Park**. (Rex Nye photo)

The **Smith Eslick Cottage Court** is over 100 years old. (Grand Lake Area Historical Society)

The **Temple Pavilion** has antique ranching & rodeo displays. (High Country Stampede & Rodeo)

YOUR HISTORY FRIENDS

We are the Grand County Historical Association. This A to Z alphabet book is one of our important projects. Our four museums sponsor many history programs. In 1974, our Pioneer Village Museum began in the original 1924 Hot Sulphur Springs Schoolhouse. Later, the original county courthouse (1891-1902), and county jail (1897-1937), a blacksmith shop, the Horseshoe Ranger Station converted to a 1900's ranch house, the 8-Mile School (1920-1942), outdoor displays, and an archive research center were added.

Our Cozens Ranch Museum invites you to see Grand County's first stage stop and Fraser's first post office. Cozens Ranch is listed on the National Register of Historic Places.

In Granby, our Emily Warner Field Aviation Museum is in the former Rocky Mountain Airways airline terminal featuring airport and aviation history.

In Kremmling, our Heritage Park Museum boasts outdoor displays and six historic buildings: the McElroy Livery Barn which is on the Colorado Register of Historic Sites, the Hermitage Ranch House, a 1915 Forest Service Ranger Station, the Ritschard Family fishing cabin, plus the original Kremmling town jail, and old railroad depot.

Stop by and see your history friends soon. Learn more about the Grand County Historical Association at www.grandcountyhistory.org

www.ingramcontent.com/pod-product-compliance
Lightning Source LLC
Chambersburg PA
CBHW062012090426
42811CB00005B/831